What is a Snail?

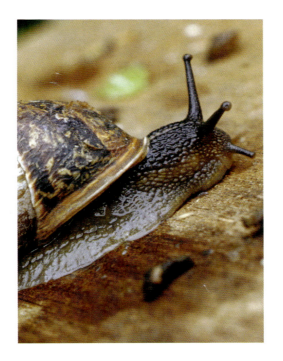

written by Pam Holden

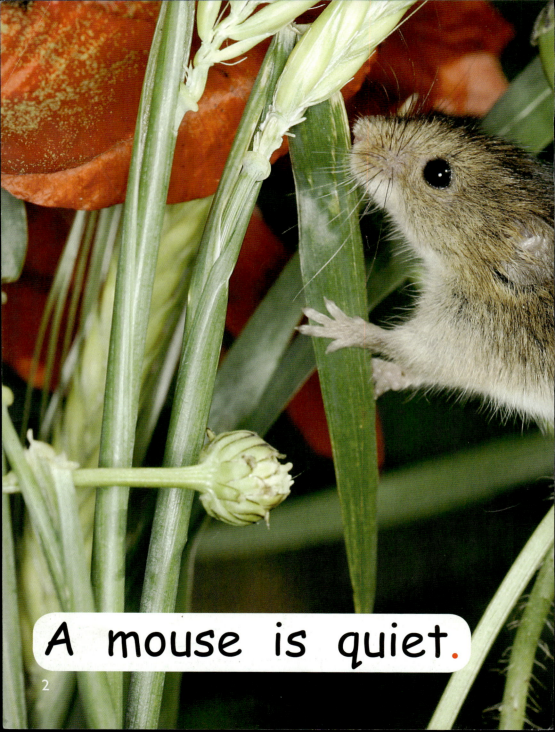

A mouse is quiet.

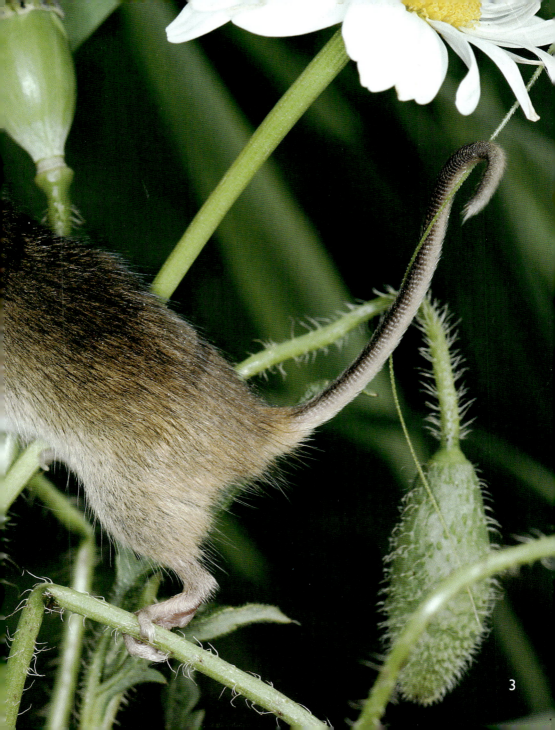

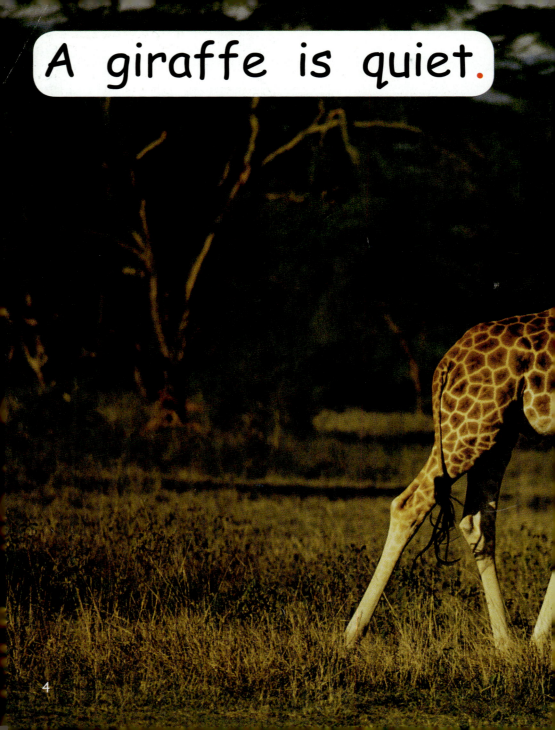

A giraffe is quiet.

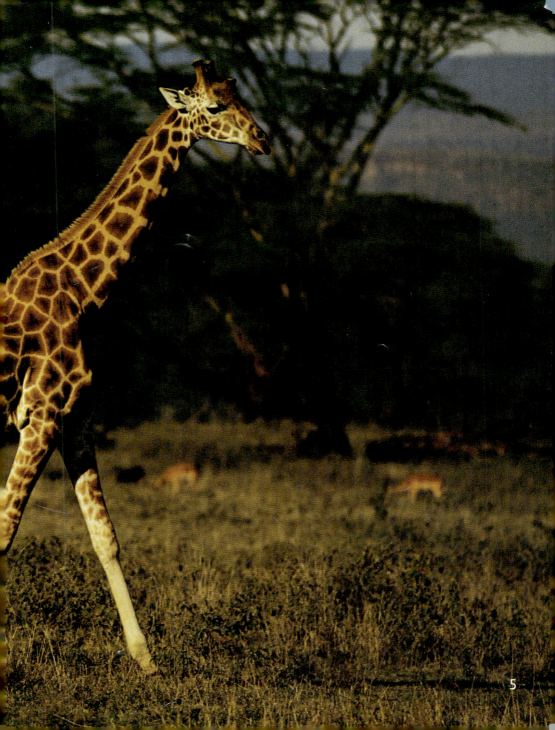

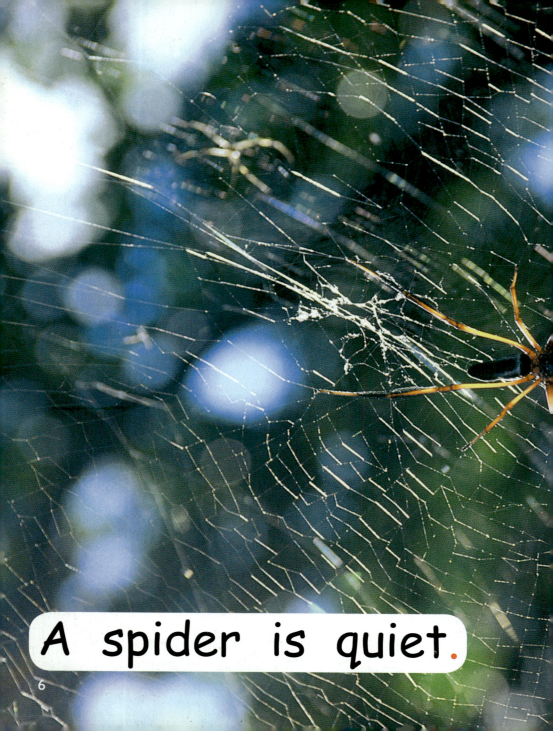

A spider is quiet.

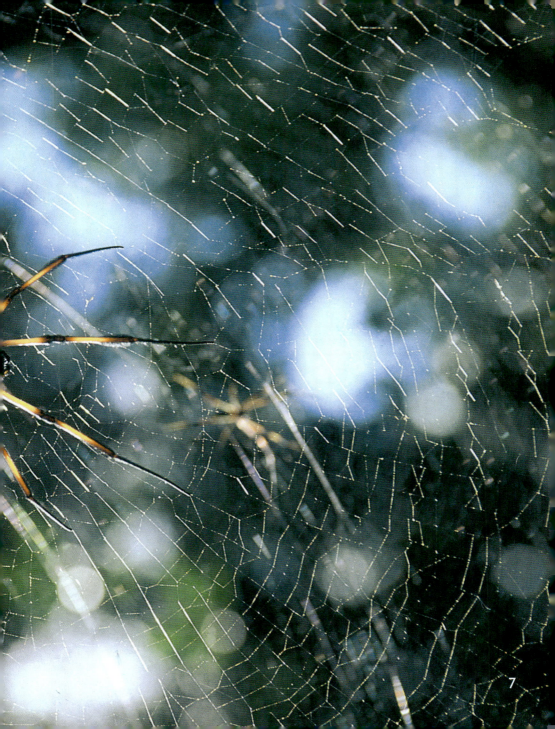

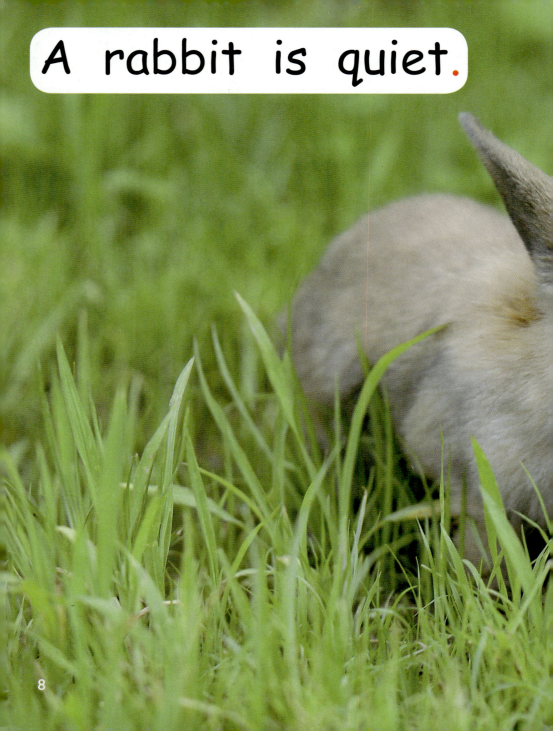
A rabbit is quiet.

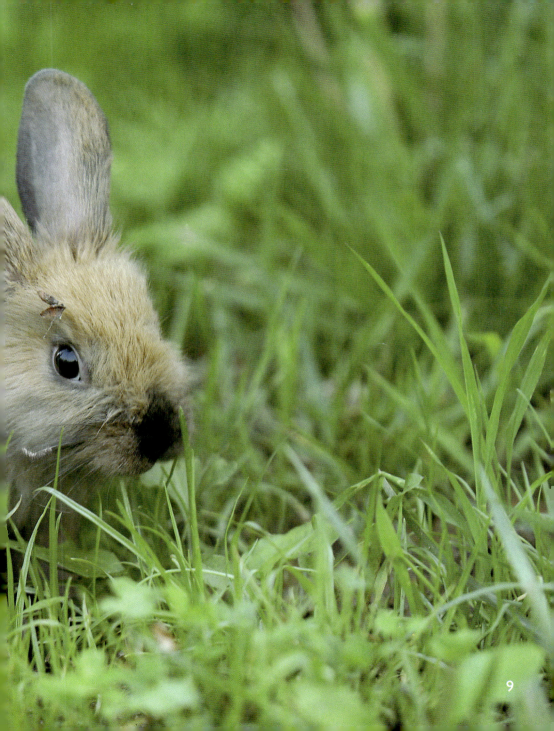

A snail is quiet.

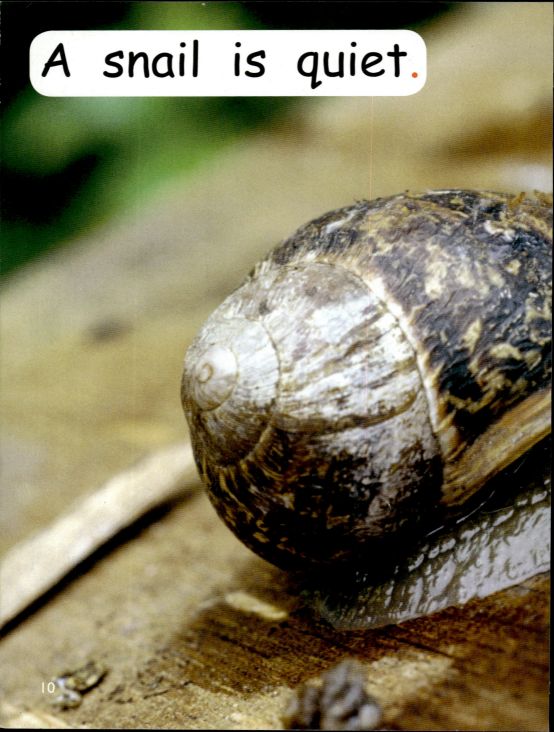

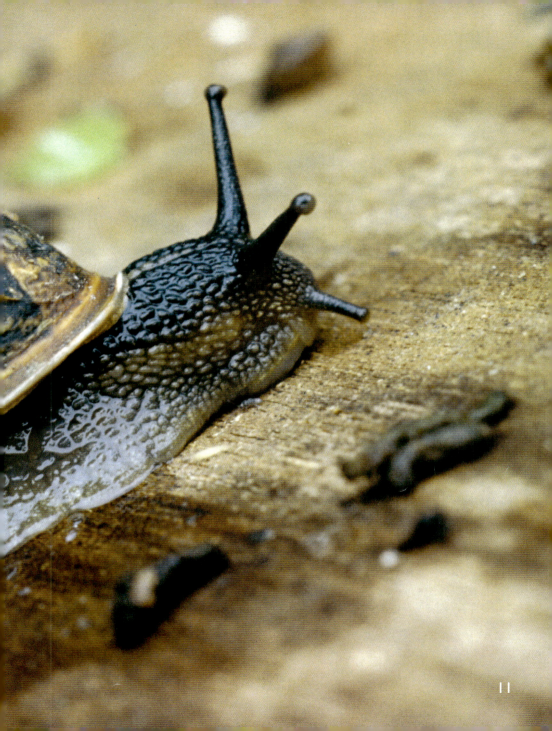

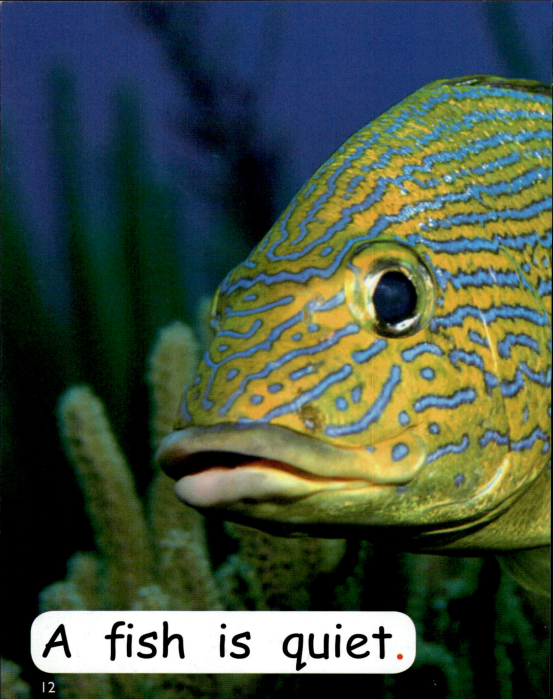

A fish is quiet.

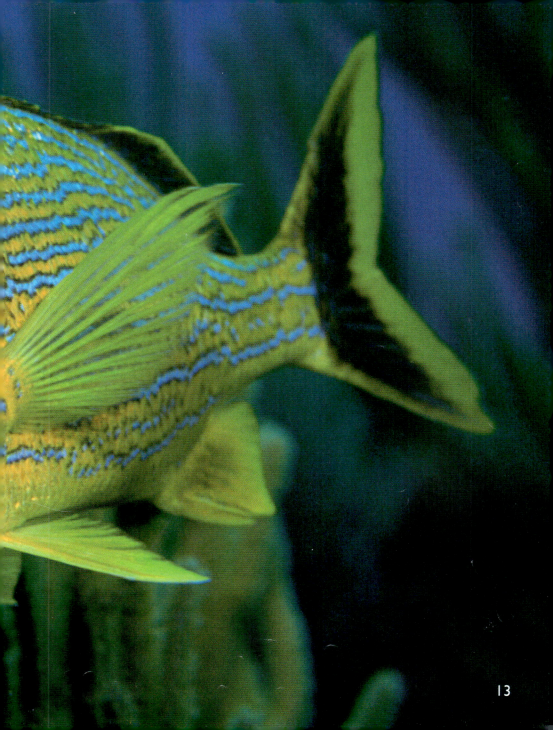

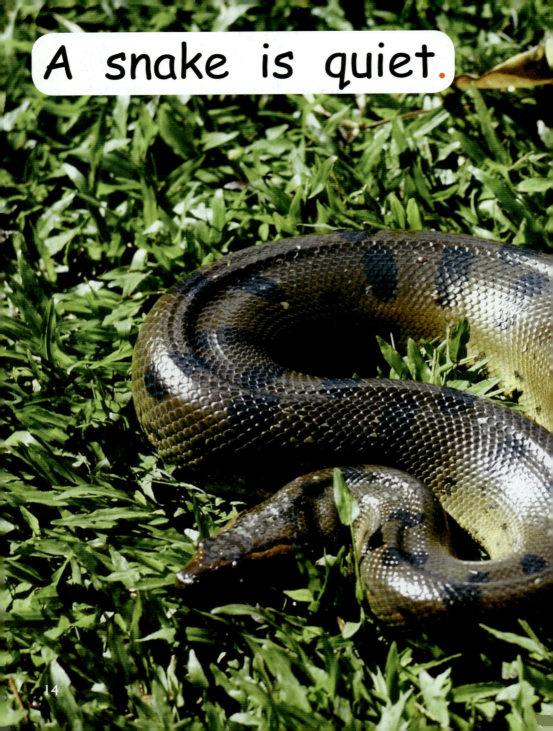

A snake is quiet.

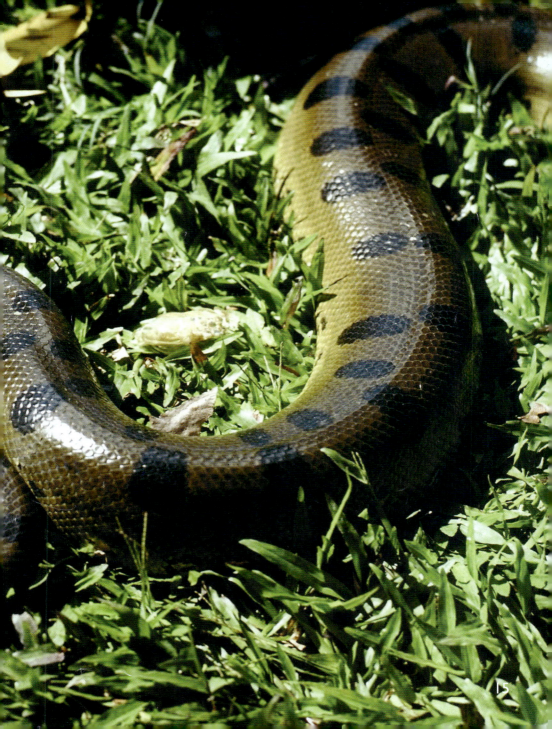

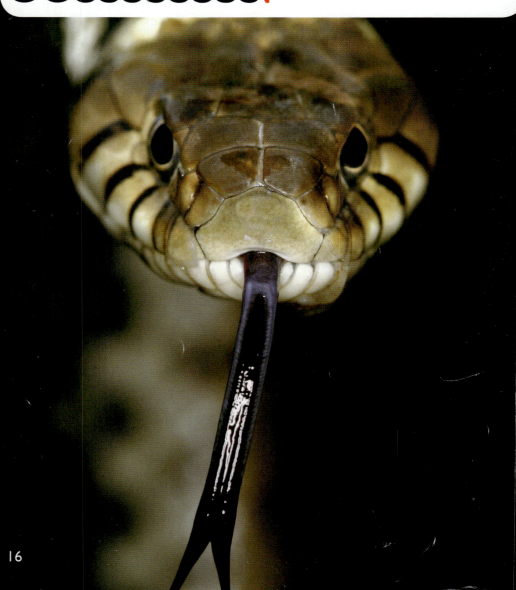

A snake is not quiet!
SSsssssssss!